MOUNTAIN LIONS

Published by Smart Apple Media
1980 Lookout Drive, North Mankato, Minnesota 56003

Design and Production by The Design Lab/Kathy Petelinsek

Photographs by D. Robert & Lorrie Franz, Leonard Rue Enterprises, McDonald Wildlife,
Tom Stack & Associates, Tom Ulrich, Visuals Unlimited

Library of Congress Cataloging-in-Publication Data
Wrobel, Scott.
Mountain lions / by Scott Wrobel
p. cm. – (Northern Trek)
Includes resources, glossary, and index
Summary: Describes the behavior, habitat, physical characteristics, endangered status,
and conservation of the North American mountain lion.
ISBN 1-58340-035-4
1. Pumas–Juvenile literature. [1. Pumas. 2. Endangered species.] I. Title.
II. Series: Northern Trek (Mankato, Minn.)

QL737.C23W758   2000
599.75'24–dc21   98-51601

2 4 6 8 9 7 5 3

NORTHERN TREK

MOUNTAIN LIONS

WRITTEN BY SCOTT WROBEL

SMART APPLE MEDIA

The mountain lion is unique to the North American continent.

Early settlers, from as far back as the 1500s, wrote of hearing this elusive

animal "screaming" from the woods. Rarely, however, did people actually

see the cat. Instead, they imagined the noises they were hearing from the

dark forests came from some sort of monster. Settlers were frightened,

and people remained wary of the mountain lion even after it was seen

and identified. For many people today, a fear of this wild cat remains.

UNLIKE THE LION

of Africa and the Bengal tiger of South Asia, the mountain lion (*Felis concolor*) is not considered a "big cat." Rather, the mountain lion, often also called a cougar, panther, or puma, is a "small cat," distinctly North American. This slender animal with strong, lanky shoulders is actually closely related to the domestic cat. Both of these cat species purr when content and lack the roaring ability of lions and tigers. The voice box of smaller cats allows only hissing and screeching.

Though smaller than the big cats, mountain lions are still among the largest **predators** on the continent. A female mountain lion generally weighs between 100 and 140 pounds (45-63 kg) and can measure more than seven feet (2.1 m) from head to tail. An adult male can weigh up to 200 pounds (91 kg) or more and may stand three feet (0.9 m) tall at the shoulder.

The mountain lion's body is built for hunting.

Mountain lions are strong climbers. They can even jump more than 15 feet (4.5m) from the ground into a tree.

The cat can retract its claws into huge, soft paws, allowing it to run or **stalk** silently. Its muscular hind legs, which are longer than its front legs, enable it to pounce as far as 20 feet (6 m) from a still position, and its long tail acts as a weight to give the cat balance as it stalks slowly close to the ground. The lion's large, black-tipped ears can rotate around to trace the slightest sound, and its eyes have **binocular vision**, which allows the lion to accurately judge distances.

The mountain lion's hunting technique is similar to that of a house cat sneaking up on a bird or a mouse. The lion stalks its prey—usually deer—by quietly crawling forward in a low crouch with

The mountain lion's only enemies are wolves, grizzly bears, wolverines, and humans, placing it near the top of nature's food chain.

By targeting weak or sick animals, mountain lions help deer, elk, and other prey animals succeed in nature. During the winter especially, when food is scarce, stronger animals survive to better sustain their populations.

its eyes fixed on the prey. When the cat is within striking distance, its eyes widen and it springs through the air to seize the throat of the surprised animal in its strong jaws. When the brief struggle ends, the mountain lion may have enough food to last a week.

No matter how large the prey, the mountain lion may drag the **carcass** a mile away to a safe hiding place where it can eat in peace. Depending on the availability of prey, mountain lions may need to

Mountain lions don't like to swim, but they will sometimes catch fish in shallow streams and lakes. Their most valuable food supply is deer meat.

If food is scarce, a mountain lion may travel 30 to 50 miles (48-80 km) in search of prey. It will usually weave back and forth across its territory, not staying in one spot for too long.

kill one to three times a week. Unlike many cats, which tend to hunt at night, mountain lions are active for most of the day. A single lion's hunting **territory** may be between 100 and 150 square miles (259-388 km²). Its main food source is deer, but the mountain lion also preys on wild hogs, rabbits, rodents, elk, bighorn sheep, raccoons, and smaller predators. Although they are superb hunters, the cats are quiet, nonaggressive animals that kill only to eat.

Mountain lions are solitary creatures that spend most of their days hunting alone, but they must gather together for **breeding**. The breeding season for mountain lions is year-round. A female breeds once every two or three years. As soon as a female mountain lion has found a partner and mated, she chooses a dry, safe place for a den, such as a cave, a walled rocky area, or a dense thicket. Three to four months later, she gives birth to a litter of one to five cubs.

Mountain lion cubs, like house cats, are born blind and are totally dependent on their mothers for survival. Cubs are not born with the solid tawny-brown coat of adults; instead, their coats are spotted with brown, and their tails have dark rings around them. This pattern helps the young lions to blend into their surroundings and hide from predators. The cubs demand a constant supply of milk

Cubs begin to travel and hunt with their mother when they reach about three months of age. They will stay with her until they are nearly two years old.

and **nurse** for about nine weeks until their jaws are strong enough to eat meat. Mountain lions usually live up to 12 years, and it is not unusual for a female to give birth to three to five litters in her lifetime.

Although many Native Americans saw the mountain lion as a noble, courageous creature, most of the white settlers who moved west in the 1800s saw the cat as a dangerous livestock killer and threat to humans. Around 1900, mass mountain lion hunts became a national sport, just as buffalo hunts were decades earlier. Predator control became a national mission, and hunters and trappers slaughtered thousands of mountain lions and other predators such as coyotes and wolves. Today,

When it reaches about three years of age, the mountain lion will be fully mature and will have claimed a territory of its own.

only about 6,500 mountain lions are left in the western and southwestern United States.

The mountain lion's **habitat** originally stretched from northern Canada to South America. But by the middle of the 20th century, the lion had been forced from most wooded regions. Today, the only places that offer suitable habitat for mountain lions are the most remote areas of the American West: the back

A mountain lion leaves piles of droppings and urinates on trees to mark its territory. Other lions who don't heed the warning to "stay out" may end up in a fight.

country of the Rocky Mountains and the deserts of the Southwest. These regions provide the stealthy cats with cover—foliage, rock formations, boulders, or canyons—that allows them to hide while stalking prey.

The only way to protect the mountain lion is to provide it with plenty of wild habitat and to keep human interference to a minimum. In the 1990s, mountain lion hunting remained legal—though controlled—in most western American states and sections of Canada. Many organizations, such as the Sierra Club, continue to work to insure that mountain lions and other wild predators receive legal protection from hunters and land developers.

Its ability to breed year-round, coupled with its knack for avoiding people, has allowed the

majestic mountain lion to survive into the 21st century despite humans' earlier efforts to eliminate it. Through the educational efforts of many conservation organizations, more people are beginning to see the value of the mountain lion, both as a beautiful creature and a necessary part of nature's life cycle.

To protect mountain lions in the future, scientists must continue to study wild habitats. They need to understand how mountain lions, their prey, and humans all live together in the same areas year after year.

UNLIKE MANY LARGE wild animals, such as buffalo or elk, it is rare for the general public to view a mountain lion in its natural habitat. The best viewing areas are zoos or wildlife parks such as Bear Country U.S.A., which is located outside Rapid City, South Dakota.

The mountain lion is among the most widely distributed wild predators in North America. Listed here are some mountain lion habitats with adequate public access. As with any trek into nature, it is important to remember that wild animals are unpredictable and can be dangerous if approached. The best way to view wildlife is from a respectful—and safe—distance.

THE ROCKY MOUNTAIN REGION *The Rocky Mountain Region includes Banff and Waterton Lakes National Parks, which are both in Alberta, Canada; Glacier National Park in Montana; Yellowstone and Grand Teton National Parks in Wyoming; and Rocky Mountain National Park in Estes Park, Colorado. All six parks have interpretive centers with a great deal of information about their current mountain lion populations.*

THE BIG HORN MOUNTAINS OF WYOMING AND MONTANA *The Bighorn National Forest offers a great deal of public access, including camping and hiking. Of the areas listed, this is the area least frequented by tourists, so your chances of seeing a mountain lion, though still rare, increase greatly.*

THE SONORAN DESERT OF ARIZONA *This region of the Southwest includes Grand Canyon and Arches National Parks, and also the Apache, Santa Fe, Prescott, and Kaibab National Forests. All of these areas have documented mountain lion populations, and the majority of the nation's sport hunting for mountain lions occurs in this region of the country.*

binocular vision: *sight that uses both eyes to look in the same direction*

breeding: *mating between a male and female animal to produce offspring*

carcass: *the body of a dead animal*

habitat: *a place or environment where a plant or animal normally lives*

nurse: *to drink milk from a mother animal*

predators: *animals that kill other animals for food*

stalk: *to hunt an animal by sneaking up on it*

territory: *the area of land that is claimed by an animal*